*S*erenity of *H*eart
Bearing the Troubles of This Life

Also available from
Sophia Institute Press
by St. Francis de Sales:

Thy Will Be Done:
Letters to Persons in the World

Serenity of Heart

Bearing the Troubles of This Life

by St. Francis de Sales

SOPHIA INSTITUTE PRESS®
Manchester, New Hampshire

Serenity of Heart is an excerpt from *The Spiritual Conferences,* a collection of St. Francis de Sales's conferences delivered to the Visitation Sisters, translated from the French by Abbot Gasquet and Canon Mackey, O.S.B. (London: Burns & Oates, Ltd., Benziger Brothers, 1906). *Serenity of Heart* contains extensive editorial revisions and improvements in the translation.

The cover artwork is a detail from *The Virgin Adoring the Child Jesus* by Pietro Perugino.

Sophia Institute Press®
Box 5284, Manchester, NH 03108
1-800-888-9344
website: http:\\www.sophiainstitute.com

Library of Congress Cataloging-in-Publication Data

Francis, de Sales, Saint, 1567-1622
   [Vrays entretiens spirituels. English]
   Serenity of heart : bearing the troubles of this life / by St.
     Francis de Sales.
     p.   cm.
   An excerpt from The Spiritual conferences, a collection of St.
     Francis de Sales's conferences delivered to the Visitation Sisters.
   Includes bibliographical references.
   ISBN 0-918477-63-8 (pbk. : alk. paper)
   1. Spiritual life – Catholic Church. I. Title.
   BX2179.F82V7313 1997
   248.4′82 – dc21   97-37657 CIP

97 98 99 00 01 02 10 9 8 7 6 5 4 3 2 1

Contents

1. Constancy will carry us
through life's difficulties 3

2. God will guide us on our way,
no matter how difficult it may be . . . 21

3. We must trust in
God's Providence 35

Biographical note 51

Serenity of Heart

Bearing the Troubles of This Life

1.

*Constancy
will carry us
through life's
difficulties*

*T*he great St. John Chrysostom,[1] reminds us of the inconstancy, variety, and instability of the events of this mortal life. Oh! How useful is this awareness! And it is the absence of this awareness that leads us to discouragement and inconsistency, to disquietude and changeableness, to inconstancy and instability in our resolutions. We desire not to meet with any difficulties, any contradiction, any trouble in our path; we want consolations without dryness or distaste, advantages without drawbacks, health without sickness, repose without labor, peace without troubles.

Ah! Who does not see our folly?

[1] St. John Chrysostom (c. 347-407; bishop of Constantinople, famous for his preaching and biblical interpretation), Homily 8 on the Gospel of St. Matthew, section 3.

Instability in life is inevitable

We desire what cannot be. Unmixed good or unmixed evil is only to be found in Heaven or in Hell. In Heaven, happiness, repose, and consolation exist in all their perfection, with no admixture of evil, trouble, or affliction; in Hell, on the contrary, are found evil, despair, trouble, and disquietude, without any admixture of good, hope, tranquillity, or peace.

But in this perishable life, good is never to be found without evil following in its train: there is no wealth without anxiety, no repose without labor, no consolation without affliction, no health without sickness.

In short, good and evil are, in all things here below, mixed together and mingled; this life presents a continued variety of diverse events. Thus God has willed that the seasons should be diversified, and that summer should be followed by autumn, and winter by spring, in order to teach us that in this world "nothing is lasting,"[2] and that temporal things are perpetually mutable, inconstant, and subject to change.

Our failure to recognize this truth is, as I have said, what makes us unstable and changeable in our moods, inasmuch as we do not make use of our reason, which God has given us to render us unchanging, firm, steadfast, and hence like unto God.

Reason helps us to rise above life's instability

When God said, "Let us make man to our likeness,"[3] He thereby bestowed on him reason and the use thereof, so that he would be able to discuss and consider good and evil, distinguish one from the other, and know which things should be chosen and which rejected.

By the use of reason, man can remain firm and constant amid all the various events and

---

[2] Eccles. 2:11.
[3] Gen. 1:26.

accidents of this mortal life. Let the weather be fine or let it rain, let the air be calm or let the wind blow, the wise man pays no attention to it, knowing well that nothing in this life is stable and permanent, and that this is not a place of rest.

In affliction he does not despair but waits for consolation; in sickness he does not torment himself but waits for health, or if he sees that his illness is such that death must follow, he thanks God, hoping for the repose of the immortal life that follows upon this one. If poverty overtakes him he does not distress himself, for he knows very well that riches do not exist in this life without poverty; if he is despised, he knows well that honor here below has no permanence, but is generally followed by dishonor or contempt.

In short, in all kinds of events, in prosperity or adversity, he remains firm, steadfast, and constant in his resolution to aspire and to strain after the enjoyment of eternal blessings.

Spiritual constancy is also necessary

But we must not only consider this variety, changeableness, and instability in the transitory and material things of this mortal life; we must also consider them in their relation to the events of our spiritual life, in which firmness and constancy are all the more necessary as the spiritual life is raised above the mortal and bodily life.

God has given reason to man to guide him, yet there are very few who allow it to rule in them; on the contrary, they let themselves be governed by their passions and not by reason; therefore they are, generally speaking, inconsistent, variable, and changeable in their moods. If they have a fancy to go to bed early or very late, they do just whichever they please; if they want to get up early to go to the country, they do so; if they prefer to sleep, they do that. If they want to dine or sup early or very late, they arrange so. And not only are they inconsistent and changeable in these matters, but they are the same in their relations with others. They wish people to accommodate themselves to their moods and will not accommodate themselves to those of others. They allow themselves to be carried away by their inclinations, affections, and passions; and provided that they do not interfere much with their neighbors' tastes and ways, they are not looked upon as unreasonable or capricious. And why? For no other reason than because this is an ordinary defect among people of the world.

But in religion we must not allow ourselves to be carried away by our passions.

In what ways do we display caprice and inconstancy? It is in the changes of our tempers, wills, and desires. At present I am joyous, because all things are succeeding as I wished; very soon I shall be sad, because a little unexpected contradiction will have arisen.

But did you not know that this is not the place where pure and unalloyed pleasure is to be found, and that this life is full of such troubles? Today, because you have consolations in your prayer, you feel encouraged and thoroughly resolved to serve God; but tomorrow, when dryness comes upon you, you will have no heart for the service of God: "Alas!" you say, "I am so languid and dejected!"

Reason enables us to develop spiritual constancy

But come now, tell me: if you governed yourself by reason, would you not see that if it was good to serve God yesterday, it is still very good to serve Him today, and will equally be very good to do so tomorrow? He is always the same God, as worthy of being loved in dryness as in consolation.

Today we desire one thing and tomorrow another; what I see done by so-and-so at this moment pleases me, but presently it will displease me so greatly that I might even conceive an aversion for that person. Just now I love someone very much, and take great delight in his conversation; tomorrow, I shall scarcely be able to endure him.

And why? Is he not as worthy of being loved today as he was yesterday?

If we attended to the dictates of reason, we should see that this person ought to be loved because he is a creature who bears the image of the divine Majesty; and thus we should take as much pleasure in his conversation now as we did formerly.

But all this inconstancy proceeds from the fact that we allow ourselves to be guided by our inclinations, our passions, or our affections, thus perverting the order placed in us by God, which requires that all should be subject to reason. For if reason does not dominate all our powers, faculties, passions, inclinations, affections, and indeed all that makes up our being, what will be the result, if not a continual state of vicissitude, inconstancy, variety, changeableness, and inconsistency that will make us at this moment fervent, and shortly afterward lazy, careless, and

idle; at one moment joyous, at the next melancholy? We shall be calm for an hour, and then
uneasy for two days. In short, our life will pass
away in idleness and waste of time.

We must resolve to be constant

Let us, then, consider the inconstancy and
uncertainty of success both in temporal and
spiritual things, so that in the event of sudden
occurrences, which from being quite new and
unforeseen might give a shock to our minds, we
may not lose courage, nor suffer ourselves to be
carried away by unevenness of temper amid the
unevenness of things that happen to us. Rather,
submitting to the guidance of the reason that
God has implanted in us, and to His Providence,
let us remain firm, constant, and unchangeable
in the resolution we have made to serve God
steadfastly, bravely, boldly, and fervently, without any interruption whatsoever.

If I were speaking to people who did not
understand me, I should try to impress upon

them, as much as I could, what I have just been saying. But you know very well that I have always tried to bring before you this most holy evenness of mind as the special and most necessary virtue of religion. All the ancient fathers of religious orders have done their utmost to make this evenness and steadfastness of mind and temper reign in their monasteries. For this end they established statutes, constitutions, and rules, in order that the religious might make use of them as a bridge by which to pass from the constant uniformity of the exercises marked out in them and to which they have subjected themselves, to this most lovable and desirable evenness of spirit amid all the changes and contrarieties that are to be met with on the path of our mortal as well as of our spiritual life.

Even the Holy Family
endured troubles

The great St. John Chrysostom says: O man, you who are so much disquieted because all things do not succeed according to your wishes, are you not ashamed to see that what you want was not to be found even in the family of our Lord?

Consider, I pray you, the vicissitudes and changes, and alternations of joy and sorrow, which are to be met with there. Our Lady received the tidings that she would conceive of the Holy Spirit a Son, who would be our Lord and Savior. What joy, what jubilation for her in that sacred hour of the Incarnation of the Eternal Word! Shortly afterward St. Joseph, seeing that she was with child and knowing that it was not by him – alas! into what affliction, into what distress was he not plunged! And our Lady, what an extremity of grief and pain did she not feel in her soul, seeing her dear husband on the point of quitting her, her modesty not permitting her to reveal to St. Joseph the honor and the grace with which God had favored her! Then a little later, when this storm had passed over because the angel had revealed to St. Joseph the secret of this mystery, what consolation did they not receive!

When our Lady brought forth her Son, the angels announced His birth, and the shepherds and the Magi came to adore Him. I leave you to imagine what rejoicing and consolation of spirit was theirs amid all this!

But wait, for that is not all. A little later, the angel of the Lord said to St. Joseph in a dream, "Take the child and His mother and flee into Egypt, because Herod wishes to put the child to death."[4] Oh, without doubt, how great a cause of grief must not this have been to our Lady and St. Joseph! How exactly the angel treats St. Joseph as a true religious! "Take the child," he says, "and His mother, and flee into Egypt, and remain there until I tell thee." What is all this? Might not poor St. Joseph have said: "You tell me to go; will it not be time enough to go tomorrow morning? Whither would you

[4] Matt. 2:13.

16

have me go by night? My preparations are not made; how would you have me carry the child? Will my arms be strong enough to carry Him all through so long a journey? Or perhaps you mean His mother to carry Him in her turn? Alas! Do you not see that she is but a young girl, weak and tender? I have neither horse nor money for this journey. And do you not know that the Egyptians are enemies to the Israelites? Who will receive us?"

Had we been in St. Joseph's place, should we not have urged a thousand such pleas to excuse ourselves from obeying the command? Whereas he did not say a word to excuse himself from doing his duty, but set out at that very moment on his journey, and did all that the angel had commanded him.

Our response to God's inspirations must be prompt

There are many useful remarks to be made regarding this command. In the first place, we are taught that in matters of obedience, there must be no putting off, no delay. It is the act of the slothful to delay, and to say as St. Augustine said of himself, "By-and-by, yet a little," and then I will be converted.[5]

The Holy Spirit will have no putting off, but desires great promptitude in obeying His inspirations. Our slothfulness, which makes us say, "I will begin presently," is our destruction.

Why not now, at this very moment, when He is inspiring and urging us?

It is because we are so tender over ourselves that we are afraid of all that seems likely to take away our repose, which is really nothing but our slothfulness and indolence. We do not wish to be roused by any external objects that would draw us out of ourselves, and we say like the sluggard, who, when his friends tried to induce him to come out of his house, thus complained, "How can I? There is a lion in the way and

[5] St. Augustine, *Confessions,* Bk. 8, ch. 5.

bears are round about, which will certainly devour me."[6]

Oh, how very wrong we are to let God press and knock again and again on the door of our hearts, before we will open to Him and permit Him to enter in and dwell there![7] Alas! It is much to be feared that we shall excite His anger and compel Him to abandon us.

Peace is a fruit of constancy

Further, we must consider the great peace and serenity of mind of the Blessed Virgin and St. Joseph, shown in their constancy amid all the unexpected events that, as we have said, befell them. Now consider whether we are justified in being surprised and troubled when we meet with similar problems, seeing that they occurred even in the family of our Lord, in which dwelt constancy and steadfastness itself

[6] Cf. Prov. 22:13; 26:13.
[7] Rev. 3:20.

in the person of our Lord. We must repeat
over and over again to ourselves, so as the better
to impress the truth upon our minds, that no
disturbance of events must ever carry away our
hearts and minds into unevenness of temper;
for unevenness of temper proceeds from no
other source than our passions, inclinations,
or unmortified affections. These must have no
power over us whenever they incite us to do,
to omit, or to desire anything, however small,
which is contrary to what the dictates of reason
urge us to do or leave undone in order to
please God.

2.

*God will guide
  us on our way,
no matter how
difficult it may be*

*T*he angel of the Lord said to St. Joseph: "Take the child and His mother, and flee into Egypt, and remain there until I tell thee." Dwell on this expression, "the angel of the Lord," and observe how highly we ought to esteem the care, succor, assistance, and direction of those whom God places about us in order to help us walk surely in the way of perfection.

Notice, in the first place, that when we say "the angel of the Lord," it must not be understood in the same sense as when we speak of our guardian angel, appointed by God to take care of us. Our Lord, who is the King and Leader of the very angels themselves, has no need – that is, never in His mortal life had need – of a guardian angel. When, therefore, we say "the angel of the Lord," we mean the angel appointed to the care of the household

and family of our Lord, and especially devoted
to His service and to that of the Blessed Virgin.

Our journey through
life is full of dangers

To explain this in a familiar manner: St.
Gregory[8] says that in this miserable world, if
we wish to keep firm and steadfast in the work
we have undertaken of saving or perfecting ourselves, we should behave like people who walk
on ice. For these, says he, take each other by the
hand or under the arms, so that if one of them
slips, the other may hold him up, and that other,
when he in his turn is on the point of falling,
may be held up by his friend.

We in this life are walking, as it were, on the
ice, exposed at each moment to the danger of
meeting with occasions of slipping and of falling,
now into vexation, now into murmurings, soon

---

[8] St. Gregory Thaumaturgus ("the Wonderworker";
c. 213-270, Greek Church father), Paraphrase of
Ecclesiastes, ch. 4, sections 10-12.

into a certain perversity, which makes us dis-
satisfied with everything that our neighbor
does. Then follows disgust for our vocation;
melancholy suggesting to us that we shall never
do any good in it, and so on through all those
troubles like these that are to be met with in
our little spiritual world.

Other persons can help
us develop constancy

Certain persons, then, are given to us to help
us keep steadily on our way, to prevent our falling, or, if we fall, to aid us in getting up again.[9]
Oh! With what openness, cordiality, sincerity,
simplicity, and faithful confidence ought we not
to converse with these persons, who are given
to us by God to help us in our spiritual progress.

---

[9] St. Francis de Sales is speaking about the spiritual
directors and superiors in a religious order; his
words generally apply as well to laypersons, who
have priests, parents, and others to help them keep
steadily on their spiritual way.

Certainly we should act toward them as
we would toward our guardian angels, because
they are commissioned to help us by their inspirations, to defend us in perils, to reprove us
when we err, and to exhort us to the pursuit
of virtue. They are charged with carrying our
prayers before the throne of the majesty, good-
ness, and mercy of our Lord, and to bring back
to us the answers to our petitions. The graces,
too, that God wishes to bestow upon us, He
gives through the intervention or intercession
of our good angels.

Now, those persons who aid us are our visible good angels, just as our holy guardian angels
are our invisible ones. These persons do visibly
what our good angels do inwardly; for they
warn us of our faults; they encourage us when
we are weak and languid; they encourage us in
our endeavors to attain perfection; they prevent
us from falling by their good counsels, and they
help us to rise up again, when we have fallen
over some precipice of imperfection or fault.

If we are overwhelmed with weariness
and disgust, they help us to bear our trouble
patiently, and they pray God to give us strength
to bear it so that we will not be overcome by
temptation. See, then, how much we ought to
value their assistance and care for us.

The Holy Family is a model of submission to authority

Let us now consider why our Lord, who is
the Eternal Wisdom, did not take care of His
family, I mean, did not inform St. Joseph or His
sweetest mother of all that was going to happen
to them.

Could He not have whispered into the ear
of His foster father, St. Joseph, "Let us go down
into Egypt, to stay there for such a time"? For it
is quite certain that He had the use of reason
from the moment of His conception in the
womb of the Blessed Virgin. But He would not
work this miracle of speaking before the time
had come.

Could He not have breathed His inspiration into the heart of His most holy mother, or of His beloved foster father, St. Joseph? Why, then, did He not do this instead of leaving the charge to the angel, who was greatly inferior to our Lady?

There is a mystery in it all. Our Lord would not in any way interfere with the office of St. Gabriel, who, having been commissioned by the eternal Father to announce the mystery of the Incarnation to the glorious Virgin, was henceforth in a manner the steward of the household and family of our Lord, to watch over them in all that might befall them of good or ill, and especially to prevent anything from happening that might shorten the mortal life of our little newborn child. For this reason he warned St. Joseph to carry Him quickly away into Egypt, to escape the tyranny of Herod, who intended to kill Him.

Our Lord did not wish to govern Himself, but allowed Himself to be carried by whoever wished to carry Him, and wherever they wished

to carry Him. It seemed as if He did not consider Himself wise enough to guide Himself
or His family, but allowed the angel to arrange
all things just as he pleased, although he had no
wisdom or knowledge to compare with that of
His divine Majesty.

We must defer to the wisdom of spiritual authorities

And now, as regards ourselves, shall we
dare to say that we can govern ourselves well,
and that we have no need of the help and direction of those whom God has given to us for our
guidance, not esteeming them, indeed, capable
enough for us?

Tell me, was the angel in any way superior
to our Lord or to our Lady? Had he a better
intellect or more judgment? By no means. Was
he more qualified for the work of guidance?
Was he endowed with any special or peculiar
grace? That could not be, seeing that our Lord
is both God and man, and that our Lady, being

His mother, had, in consequence, more grace and perfection than all the angels together. Nevertheless the angel commands and is obeyed.

But more than this, see what rank is observed in the Holy Family! No doubt it was the same as it is among sparrow hawks, where the hen rules and is superior to the male. Who could doubt for a moment that our Lady was much superior to St. Joseph, and that she had more discretion and qualities more fit for ruling than her spouse?

Yet the angel never addresses himself to her regarding anything that has to be done, either as to going or coming, or whatever it might be. Does it not seem to you that the angel commits a great indiscretion in addressing himself to St. Joseph rather than to our Lady, who is the head of the house, as possessing the treasure of the eternal Father? Had she not just reason to be offended by this proceeding and by this manner of treatment?

Doubtless she might have said to her spouse, "Why should I go into Egypt, since my Son has not revealed to me that I must go, still less has the angel spoken to me on the subject?" Yet our Lady makes no such remark; she is not in the least offended that the angel addresses himself to St. Joseph. She obeys quite simply, knowing that God has so ordained it. She does not ask why. It is sufficient for her that God wills it so, and that it is His pleasure that we should submit without hesitation. "But I am more than the angel," she might have said, "and more than St. Joseph." No such thought occurs to her.

Do you not see that God delights to deal thus with men, in order to teach them holy and loving submission? St. Peter was an old man, rough and uncultured; St. John, on the contrary, was young, gentle, and sweet in manners; yet God willed that St. Peter should guide the others and be their universal superior, and that St. John should be one of those who were ruled by and obeyed him.

What a lesson for the proud human intellect, which will not bow down to adore the secret mysteries of God and His most holy will unless it has some sort of knowledge why this or that is so! "I have a superior mind," we say, "I have more experience," and so on, giving specious reasons that are really only calculated to produce disquietude, variableness of temper, and murmuring.

Our obedience should be prompt and unquestioning

Why is this order given? To what end was that said? Why was such a thing done for this person rather than for the other? Ah! What a pity it is, to start to inquire so closely into what we see done! Why take so many pains to destroy our peace of heart?

We really need no other reason than that God wills it, and that ought to be enough for us.

But who will assure me that it is the will of God? We want God to reveal all things to us by secret inspirations. Would we wait until He sends angels to announce His will? He did not do this even to our Lady (at least not on this matter), but wished it to be made known to her by the intervention of St. Joseph, to whom she was subject as to her superior.

Perhaps we would like to be told and informed by God Himself, through ecstasies, raptures, visions, and whatnot! Such are the follies that we weave in our brains, rather than submit ourselves to follow the ordinary and most sweet method of holy submission to the guidance of those whom God has given us.

Let it, then, be enough to know that God wishes us to obey those He has placed in authority over us, without occupying ourselves with considering their capability. In this way we shall humble our minds to walk simply in the happy path of a holy and tranquil humility that will render us infinitely pleasing to God.

3.

We must trust in God's Providence

We must now pass on to the third consideration, which I have made on the command given by the angel to St. Joseph to take the child and His mother, and to go into the land of Egypt and remain there until he should bid him return. Truly the angel spoke very briefly: "Go, and do not return until I tell thee."

By this conduct of the angel to St. Joseph we are taught how we should embark on the sea of Divine Providence without store of biscuit, without oars or sculls, without sails — in a word, without preparing anything at all, leaving to our Lord all the care of ourselves and the result of our affairs, without doubts or questionings or fears as to what may happen.

For the angel simply says, "Take the child and His mother, and flee into Egypt," without telling

St. Joseph either by what route to journey, or what preparations they must make for the way, or into what part of Egypt they should go, or how they should be fed when they arrived there, or who would receive them.

Would not poor St. Joseph have had some reason to reply to the angel, "You tell me to depart; must it be at once?" "Instantly."

This shows us the promptitude that the Holy Spirit requires of us when He says, "Arise, come forth out of thyself and such an imperfection." How great an enemy is the Holy Spirit to all procrastination and delay!

We must not question Providence

Consider, I entreat you, the great patron and model, holy Abraham. See how God deals with him: "Abraham, go forth out of thy country and from thy kindred; and go to the mountain that I shall show thee."[10]

[10] Gen. 12:1; 22:2.

"Thou sayest, O Lord, that I must go forth
from the city; but tell me, then, in what direction I must go — to the east or to the west?"
The patriarch makes no such reply, but instantly
sets forth, and goes whither the Spirit of God
leads him, until he reaches a mountain that was
afterward called the "Vision of God,"[11] because
there he received great and marvelous graces, to
prove how pleasing promptness in obedience is
to Him.

Might not St. Joseph have said to the angel,
"Thou hast told me to take the child and His
mother; tell me then, please, how I am to feed
them on the journey; for Thou knowest well,
my Lord, that we have no money." Nothing
of all this did he say, but was absolutely confi-
dent that God would provide for everything, as
indeed He did, although sparsely, giving them
the means of subsisting in a simple way, either
by St. Joseph's trade or the alms bestowed upon

[11] Gen. 22:14.

them. Certainly they were admirable in their confidence that God would always provide what they might need for their support, leaving the whole care of themselves to Divine Providence.

We must entrust our spiritual lives to God

I consider, however, that we are not only required to rest on Divine Providence in all that concerns temporal matters, but still more in all that belongs to our spiritual life and to our perfection. It is certainly only the excessive care we take of ourselves that makes us lose our tranquillity of mind and ruffles our unsteady temper. For as soon as any contradiction arises, or if we only notice in ourselves some small sign of an unmortified spirit, or if we commit the most trifling fault, it seems to us that all is lost.

Is it so great a wonder that we sometimes find ourselves stumbling on the path of our perfection? "But I am so miserable, so full of imperfections!" Do you really recognize that?

Then thank God for having given you such knowledge, and do not lament so much: you are most happy indeed in knowing your own absolute misery. After having thanked God for this knowledge, cut off at once the useless softness that makes you complain of your infirmity.

Spiritual desolation should not discourage us

We are far too tender over our bodies, but incomparably more so over our souls, and this tenderness in both cases is very contrary to perfection. "I am not faithful to our Lord, and therefore I have no consolation in prayer." What a pity, to be sure! "But I am so often dry and cold that I think I cannot be in God's favor, since He is so full of consolation." Truly, that is well said! As if God always gave consolation to His friends!

Were there ever creatures more worthy of being loved, or more actually loved by God, than our Lady and St. Joseph, and did they always have consolations? Could a greater affliction be imagined than that experienced by St. Joseph when he knew that the glorious Virgin was with child, and not by him? His affliction and distress were all the greater, as the passion of love is more vehement than the other passions of the soul. Moreover, in love, jealousy is the extremity of its pain, as the Bride in the Song of Solomon declares, "Love is strong as death," for love produces the same effects on the soul as death does on the body; but "jealousy is hard as Hell."[12]

We must be calm in disturbances

I leave you, then, to imagine what was the grief of poor St. Joseph and of our Lady also when she saw what he whom she loved so dearly, and by whom she knew herself to be so dearly loved, must think of her.

[12] Song of Sol. 8:6.

Jealousy made St. Joseph full of irresolution.
Not knowing what course to take, he deter-
mined, rather than to blame her whom he had
always honored and loved so much, to quit her
and depart without saying a word.

"But," you will say, "I feel strongly the
trouble that this temptation or my imperfection
causes me." Very likely, but is it to be compared
to that of which we have just been speaking?
It is impossible. And if it is, ask, then, I pray
you, whether we are justified in complaining
or lamenting, when St. Joseph never complains
at all, nor gives the slightest outward sign of
disturbance. There is no bitterness of speech,
no severity of look or behavior toward our
Lady; he simply bears his trouble, and will not
take any other step except that of leaving her.
What, indeed, could he do in this matter?

But you will say, "I have such an antipathy
toward this particular person that I can hardly
speak to her without great difficulty, so displeas-
ing is conversation with her to me." Never

mind, you must disregard your antipathy and not be cross with her, as if she could help it. You must behave like our Lady and St. Joseph: you must be calm in the midst of your annoyance, and leave to our Lord the care of removing it when it pleases Him. It was in our Lady's power to appease that tempest, but she would not do it, leaving the issue of the affair wholly to Divine Providence.

We must entrust to God our efforts to perfect ourselves

The two strings of the lute that are the most different from each other, and yet the most necessary to harmonize, are the treble and the bass. The high and the low are the most opposed, yet unless these two strings are in perfect tune, the music of the lute cannot be pleasant.

In the same way, in our spiritual lute there are two things that are equally opposed, and yet both are equally necessary to be brought into harmony: to be very careful about perfecting ourselves and yet to have no care at all about our perfection, but to leave it entirely to God.

By this I mean that we must take the care that God wishes us to take about perfecting ourselves, and yet leave the care of arriving at perfection entirely to Him. God wishes our care to be a calm and peaceful one, which shall make us do whatever is judged to be fitting by those who guide us, and always proceed faithfully along the road marked out for us by the rules and directors given to us. For the rest, God wishes us to repose in His fatherly care, trying as far as is possible to keep our soul at peace, for "the place of God is in peace"[13] and in the peaceful and restful heart.

A calm soul reflects God's image

You know that when the lake is very calm, and when the winds do not agitate its waters, on a very serene night, the sky with all its stars is

[13] Ps. 75:3 (Revised Standard Version: Ps. 76:2).

so perfectly reflected in it, that looking down into its depths the beauty of the heavens is as clearly visible as if we looked up on high. So when our soul is perfectly calm, unstirred, and untroubled by the winds of superfluous cares, unevenness of spirit, and inconstancy, it is very capable of reflecting in itself the image of our Lord.

But when the soul is troubled, tossed, and agitated by the tempests of the passions, and when we allow ourselves to be governed by them, and not by the reason that makes us like unto God, then we are wholly incapable of reflecting the lovely and beloved image of our crucified Lord, or the variety of His excellent virtues.

We must therefore leave the care of ourselves to the mercy of Divine Providence, and yet at the same time do simply and cheerfully all that is in our power to amend and perfect ourselves, always taking careful heed not to allow our minds to be troubled and disquieted.

Trust in God requires ready obedience to Him

The angel told St. Joseph to remain in Egypt until he would bid him return, and this glorious saint never replied, "At what time, Lord, wilt Thou bid me do so?" This was to teach us that when we are asked to take up some duty, we must not say, "Will it be for a long time?"

Instead we must take it up quite simply, imitating the perfect obedience of Abraham when God commanded him to sacrifice his son.[14] Abraham made no reply, complaint, or delay in fulfilling God's command.

Therefore because God was satisfied with Abraham's goodwill, He showed him great favor, directing him to find a ram, which Abraham sacrificed on the mountain instead of his son.

[14] Gen. 22:1-13.

We must not fear the
difficult things God asks of us

Let me conclude by calling your attention
to the simplicity practiced by St. Joseph when,
at the command of the angel, he went down
into Egypt, a country in which he well knew
that he would find as many enemies as there
were inhabitants. Might he not have said, "Thou
commandest me to take the child away from
here, but in fleeing from one enemy Thou dost
put us into the hands of thousands of others
whom we shall meet with in Egypt, seeing that
we are Israelites." But no, he makes no reflec-
tion of any sort upon the command, and so sets
forth on his way full of peace and of confidence
in God.

In like manner, when any charge is given to
us, let us not say: "Alas! I am so impulsive; if
this charge is given to me I shall commit innu-
merable acts of impatience; I am already so dis-
tracted, if I am put in such a post as that I shall

be still more so. If I were only left here I should be so modest, so quiet, so recollected."

God is always with us

Go down quite simply into Egypt, into the midst of all the enemies whom you will find there. God, who sends you thither, will also preserve you, and you will not die in that land. But if, on the contrary, you remain in Israel, where there is also an enemy, namely your self-will, it will doubtless take your life.

But it is time to leave off speaking, and so to leave you in Egypt with our Lord, who, as I believe, and many others hold, began from this time forth, when He had time left after having helped St. Joseph in some little way in his work, to make little crosses, showing thus early His fervent longing for the work of our redemption.

Biographical note

St. Francis de Sales

(1567-1622)

A Doctor of the Church and the patron saint of writers, St. Francis de Sales was remarkable "not only for the sublime holiness of life which he achieved, but also for the wisdom with which he directed souls in the ways of sanctity."[15]

The eldest of thirteen children, Francis de Sales was born in 1567 to a noble family in the French-speaking Duchy of Savoy (an area straddling present-day eastern France and western Switzerland). He received a superb education in both France and Italy. Although intended by his father for a diplomatic career, St. Francis was ordained to the priesthood in the diocese of Geneva in 1593.

Shortly thereafter, he was sent to the Chablais region of the Savoy on a mission to persuade

[15] Pope Pius XI, *Rerum omnium perturbationem,* 4.

those who had fallen under Calvinist influence
to return to the practice of Catholicism. St.
Francis spent four years laboring at this difficult
task, during which he suffered many indignities.
More than once he was thrown out of his lodg-
ings and had to sleep in the open air. Many
times he celebrated Mass in empty churches or
continued preaching while the congregation
walked out.

Nevertheless, his unflagging poise and kind-
ness in this mission led to its eventual success.
By the turn of the century, the majority of the
area's inhabitants had returned to the Catholic
faith.[16]

After his election as bishop of Geneva in
1602, St. Francis continued his apostolic efforts
to win souls back to the Catholic Church. At the
same time, he sought to build a broad commu-
nity of devout persons within the Church who
would live the life of Christian perfection in all

[16] Ibid., 8.

their varied states and vocations.[17] It was St. Francis's absolute conviction that "holiness is perfectly possible in every state and condition of secular life," whether one is male or female, rich or poor, single or married.[18] He expounded this view at length in his classic work *Introduction to the Devout Life*. This conviction permeates the advice he gave to the many persons from all walks of life to whom he gave spiritual direction, both in person and in letters renowned for their spiritual wisdom, their psychological insight, their graciousness, and what one scholar has called their "inspired common sense."[19]

Jane Frances Frémyot, Baroness de Chantal, is the most famous of those who came to St. Francis for spiritual direction. An aristocratic

[17] *Francis de Sales, Jane de Chantal: Letters of Spiritual Direction,* ed. Wendy M. Wright and Joseph F. Power (New York: Paulist Press, 1988), 23.

[18] Pius XI, *Rerum omnium perturbationem,* 13.

[19] Elisabeth Stopp, ed., *St. Francis de Sales: Selected Letters* (New York: Harper and Bros., 1960), 33-34.

young widow with four children, she met St. Francis in 1604. In cooperation with her, St. Francis founded the Visitation of Holy Mary in Annecy in Savoy, a congregation for unmarried and widowed women who aspired to religious life but who were not sufficiently young, healthy, or free of family ties to enter one of the more austere women's orders of the day. The Visitation eventually developed into a cloistered religious order devoted to prayer and the cultivation of the "little virtues" St. Francis praised so highly. The order flourished during St. Francis's lifetime, and afterward. St. Jane de Chantal was herself canonized in 1751.

After nearly thirty years of tireless labor on behalf of the Church and Her members, St. Francis de Sales died of a cerebral hemorrhage in Lyons, France, on December 28, 1622. He had been traveling in the entourage of the king and queen of France at the time, but rather than stay in royal quarters, he lodged in the gardener's cottage on the grounds of the Visitation

convent in that city. Fittingly for this apostle of
the little virtues, he died in that modest cottage.

St. Francis de Sales was canonized in 1665.
His feast day is celebrated on January 24.